Disclaimer

At the present time the cultivation of the marijuana plant, for either medicinal or recreational use, is an illegal act. This has not always been the case, and if there is any sanity in the world this law will one-day change! But I will not live forever, and would like to pass on the enclosed knowledge to a hopefully more fortunate generation. This book is not intended to encourage any illegal act of horticulture. Just keep it handy and a new day will dawn. *John Alexander*

A friend was reminiscing about his travel

Contents

India, and told this story.....

HE WAS BOARDING A BUS IN SOME SMALL VILLAGE, and helped a local lady load volumes of stuff aboard. They sat together. "Thank you for helping me" she said. "Perhaps I could read your palm as a token of gratitude." My friend was happy to accept. She took his hand and studied his palm. "Aha!" she smiled . "I see you are a Hashisher" He smiled back and nodded. "Well it's a good job you are" she said. "Without the use of this most beneficial plant, your life would have travelled a less enlightened road."

This is of course a reversal of attitude to mainstream thinking in western society, but I am sure there was a deep understanding in what was said. There has been a vast increase in the use of marijuana in western society, and many young people have had their attitudes changed, I think for the better, from the use of this herb. With major changes occurring in the way we live, is it any wonder that we are confused by political and social dogmas and seek alternative perspectives?

I hope this book will be of help, to those who are interested in the cultivation of this "most medicinal" of plants.

IS IT THAT LIFE CHOOSES A FATE, OR THAT FATE CHOOSES A LIFE?

Whichever it is, both life and fate seem to have chosen for me an association with the herb Marijuana. From early fumblings in the sixties to a five year stint in Hawaii during the eighties, where the production of such exotics as Kona gold, Puna buds and Maui wowie was at its height, and then back to the U.K. to continue the quest. Planting, tending and harvesting of Marijuana has been a major part of my life. I shall try in this book to share the knowledge gained in the many varied seasons that have passed.

As the book is primarily concerned with developing an exotic bud-producing plant, getting the best seed for a temperate climate is of the utmost importance. There are seed suppliers who specialise in this, but results can vary, so developing ones own seed strain is the best way to go.

The most important factor in developing a seed strain for a temperate climate such as the U.K. is to produce a plant that reaches its flowering stage at the height of the summer, when temperature is at its highest. This would be late July to the end of August.

Northern Temperate Zone.
Between latitude 30° and 60° North

Tropical Zone.
Between latitude 30° South and 30° North

Is it that life chooses a fate, or that fate chooses a life?

Obviously most exotic seeds come from a tropical or subtropical climate which, as can be seen from the illustration, is below latitude 30⁰ in the Northern Hemisphere. In these tropical latitudes, the number of hours of daylight for Midsummer would be considerably less than for the U.K.

For example in Hawaii on June 21st, which is the longest day in the Northern hemisphere, the daylight hours would be approximately 13.5 hours, whereas in Southern England the daylight hours would be approximately 18 hours.

The flowering of the Marijuana plant requires a reduction in the number of daylight hours. It is this reduction which triggers the plant into flowering mode, the plant becoming either male or female. If we were to plant our Hawaiian seed in Southern England, it wouldn't start flowering until the daylight hours were less than 13.5 hours. This would be the tail end of August, when temperatures are falling. For good flower heads (buds) to develop, a daytime temperature of around 70°f is required.

For good flower heads to develop, a daytime temperature of around 70° f is required

To summarise the adaptations the plant needs to make;

1. Change in hours of daylight.

2. Change in temperature.

So what to do? The simplest way to artificially reduce the number of daylight hours is to cover selected plants with a light-proof cover in early to mid June. If the covers were to be placed over the plants three hours before sunset and removed the following morning three hours after dawn, a total reduction of six hours daylight would be achieved. If this process were to be repeated for the next two weeks, signs of flowering would be observed. The light reduction could all be taken from one end of the day, which of course would halve the work.

If this rather repetitive task is continued until the plants are sexually mature and pollination occurs, then seeds would start to develop. It would be worth covering at least six plants to be sure of having both a male and female, and selecting the best looking of both sexes. Get rid of any weak-looking males.

It might also be necessary to pinch out the tops of the plants to keep them short. This will also tend to make them more bushy, as two growing tips will develop for every one pinched out. Start the pinching-out process after the plant has developed at least four growing nodes, and continue until signs of sexing.

It is possible to develop strains of plants that are small of stature and mature quickly, which makes them ideal for growing in a greenhouse. These can be grown in trays, as illustrated here, using a compost growing medium.

Any seed produced in the first year is the foundation for future efforts. Given a reasonable summer, plants grown outside can produce seeds in mid to late September.

The following year the early greenhouse seed produced by covering the plants, crossed with the seed produced outside, will give an earlier flowering plant. If the best looking, earliest flowering plants are always used for seed production, then year by year the flowering process will be advanced and the strain improved. Developing several varieties of seed allows for cross pollination, which prevents plants becoming inbred and weak.

Greenhouses make life a lot easier when cultivating in a temperate climate, and a greenhouse with a light-proof area under the staging is an alternative to covering the plants. The plants should be in pots or growing trays, to allow them to be easily moved.

As mentioned earlier, at the flowering stage the marijuana plant develops into either a male or female. Each seed has the potential to be either, although certain factors can tend to influence this and we will delve into these at a later stage.

The male plant tends to develop slightly ahead of the female, a tendency which I feel starts from germination. I have found that the seeds which are the first to crack and start sprouting very often become the more leggy, sparse leafed seedlings, which ultimately develop into male plants. One can never be certain of the sex of a plant during its early development, but females usually tend to be more squat and have a fuller form.

Germination

DECIDING WHEN TO START GERMINATING SEEDS WILL depend on climatic conditions. It is best to wait until spring is definitely in the air, so that when the young plants are moved to their outside location the ground has some warmth in it. Another factor is that the earlier a plant is started, the longer it will be to finishing. Conversely the later a plant is started, the faster it will finish, which when dealing with a more temperate climate is definitely an advantage.

Seeds should be of good colour. This will depend on country of origin, but varies from a light overall brown to a dark tiger stripe or speckle. Seeds that are very pale or a bit green should be avoided, as these will tend to be immature. Size as they say is not important, but knowing where seed has come from is, so trying to find the best is of prime importance. As so much sinsemilla is now produced under lights, where plants are effectively cloned, seeds are less easily found, but countries such as Mexico, Morocco, Sudan, Colombia, India, Nepal and (my personal favourite) Hawaii are but a few of the places producing good Marijuana, and good seed.

Germination is best done in a heated propagator in the following manner. Soak the seed overnight in a jam-jar filled with water, swish them about a bit to get the seeds wet, and by morning most of the seeds should have sunk to the bottom of the jar.

The propagator needs to be placed somewhere where the temperature is fairly stable. Any large variations in temperature will affect the temperature inside the propagator, which should remain at a constant 70°f. Most heated propagators are thermostatically controlled and designed to do this. As the germinating seeds are light-sensitive the propagator also needs to be kept in the shade.

Keeping everything clean is really important to prevent the introduction of disease

Prepare the propagator by placing inside it a waterproof dish, filled with a quarter-inch layer of wet absorbent matting. Strain the seeds from the jam-jar and place on the absorbent matting and cover with one more layer of matting. Make sure the matting is wet but not flooded, as it must remain at least moist through the whole germination process or the seeds will die. Replace the cover of the propagator keeping the ventilators open to allow air circulation. Keeping everything clean is really important to prevent the introduction of disease. It can happen, even to Marijuana.

The poor man's alternative to all this would be some wet loo-roll between a couple of saucers, placed in the airing cupboard .Good seed should start germinating very quickly. After two days some of the seeds should have split open as they swell, and the beginnings of tails will appear.

Remember a good proportion of these first seeds to crack will, I think, be males. If you keep a record of the order of germination you can check out this theory.

In the next couple of days more seeds should crack and the tails should develop. See page 17.

When the tails are about a quarter to a half-inch long, the seed has changed from a seed to a sprout, and It's time for them to be transferred to their growing medium.

A good system is to use five-inch peat pots filled with a medium nutrient compost. The compost should be firmed down in the pot and given a good watering before the sprouts are transferred. There are other options for the growing medium, such as a combination of one-third each of compost, Vermiculite and Perlite. Also water storage granules, available from horticultural suppliers, can be added to the mix to aid in water retention.

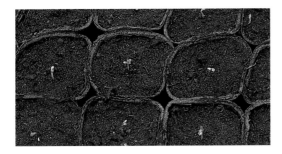

Note peat pots are in firm contact with each other to keep moisture content even.

If a Vermiculite/Perlite mix is used, then there will need to be some nutrient added to the initial watering, to compensate for what would have been in the compost. A half-strength solution of a chemical or an organic fertiliser can be used, but keep it weak or it will be like giving whisky to a baby. There are various-sized plastic trays which can be used

to contain the peat pots, but it is best if the pots are in firm contact with each other so that the moisture content is evenly distributed.

Now to transfer the sprouted seeds into their peat pots. Again it is important to keep everything very clean to prevent the introduction of disease. Make a hole in the compost large enough to take the tail of the sprouted seed, then carefully place the seed tail-down in the hole so that the seed pod itself is level with the surface of the compost. Gently firm down the surrounding compost.

Do this for all the seeds that are ready, and then continue over the next few days until all the sprouts are transferred to the peat pots.

Two points to watch for the best results;

• Make sure the temperature of the peat pots is the same as that of the sprouts in the propagator, so they suffer minimum shock during transition.

• Also make sure the tails of the sprouted seed are not damaged or broken when placing them in the compost. Be gentle!

As mentioned earlier, a greenhouse is of

great benefit when growing in a temperate climate, and a shaded spot in the greenhouse is ideal for performing the potting tasks.

During the early stages of growth the seedlings need as much light as possible. Insufficient light will cause the stems to stretch, which will weaken the plant and slow down its development, so keep them in the area of the greenhouse which gets the most light. Keeping the temperature up is also important. You are trying to give the plant as close to its natural tropical environment as possible, especially in its early development. 70° F. is an ideal daytime temperature. Using a greenhouse heater if the nights are chilly will also optimise the seedlings' development.

If a greenhouse is not available, then a south-facing window-sill or any warm, light location will do. If it's really dull during the first few days after sprouting, then the light can be supplemented by the addition of artificial light such as grow-lights or halides. Personally I have never done this, preferring instead to start several batches of seeds during the spring, and using those whose

> The less light the plants get, especially at the seedling stage, then the higher will be the proportion of males.
> The more light, the higher the proportion of females.

germination coincided with good growing conditions. My object is to try and make the plants adapt and acclimatise to the local conditions. Of course a good stock of seed is necessary to do this.

A note here about light availability, and the proportion of males to females. The less light the plants get, especially at the seedling stage, then the higher will be the proportion of males. Conversely, the more light, the higher the proportion of females. Plants can of course be started solely under artificial light, especially halide, where a very high proportion of females can be achieved. They might get a bit of a shock, when faced with the great outdoors of our more temperate climate, but with the right timing it has been known to work. It is safe to say that any sort of stress, especially during the early stages of growth, will increase the proportion of males to females.

For the first week to ten days the peat pots should be kept moist using water only, as there should be enough nutrient in the compost. (If a compost/Vermiculite/Perlite mix is being used, nutrient will have been added from the start). After this, some form of feed will have to be added to the water to keep up growth. This can be organic or chemical depending on your preference, but remember to keep it weak and don't overfeed.

It's far better to make the plant search for food. This encourages root development and prevents weak sappy growth. Use a half strength chemical or an organic alternative every second or third watering, but if the weather is poor and you want to slow down growth, then only add feed when the weather improves. If the plants are going to be transferred to an outside location it's best to keep them as stocky and strong as possible, another reason not to overfeed. A good strong root development is what is wanted at the early stage of growth.

> A good strong root development is what is wanted at the early stage of growth

After ten days to a fortnight, roots should start to break through the bottom of the pots. It is essential that the peat pots remain moist on the outside for this to happen.

When watering, pour the liquid into the tray containing the pots, rather than into the pots themselves, so that the liquid is taken up by the pots. This will encourage the roots to go down.

If you find the surface of the growing medium becomes hard and crusty, break it up with your fingers. This will allow the seedlings to breathe. Also make sure that the growing medium stays in contact with the sides of the peat pot. There is quite a lot of shrinkage as compost dries out, and a gap can form between the medium and the pot. This will of course prevent the roots from spreading and stunt growth. Should the surface of the growing medium show any signs of a white salt-like dusting, then crumble and blend the surface to remove.

If the surface of the compost has tended to be on the wet side, a green algae can develop. Again, break up the surface to remove and try to keep the compost a bit drier.

It is usually seedlings germinated early in the season, when conditions are more extreme, that require the most attention, so try to give them the best start, and make their growing medium as comfortable as possible. Although I have recommended that watering is done by adding the liquid to the bottom of the trays holding the peat pots, watering can, on occasion, be done using a very fine rose watering-can, applied to the surface of the peat pots. This will help to prevent the surface of the peat pots crusting over.

Try to apply it as a fine rain, but avoid bright sunlight as water droplets act as lenses and can burn the young tender leaves. A nutrient can be added, but again keep it very weak, no more than half-strength. The basic concept of all this technique is to try and duplicate the natural environment in which the plant is going to have to survive. So water from above with the fine rose watering-can when you decide the seedlings would like a drop of rain, otherwise top up the root system from below.

One problem that can develop, especially in damp conditions, is that the bottom of the stems are attacked by a fungus. This is known as 'damping off' and will be noticed first when a seedling keels over. On examination the base of the stem will be noticeably wasted. Treat by spraying with a fungicide, and try to keep the surface of the growing medium drier.

If conditions are damp, it is worth giving the seedlings a spray of specific fungicide as a preventative measure.

After the first two weeks, the seedlings will be developing into young plants and providing the timing has been good, some warm sunny afternoons should be happening. Find a sheltered location and let the plants have a taste of the outdoors, this will be the start of what is called 'Hardening Off'.

Find a sheltered location and let the plants have a taste of the outdoors

Get the plants out as often as possible, weather permitting. Air movement will firm up the stems and the sun will give them strength. Don't forget to bring them in at night and watch out for slugs and snails in damp weather, or you will find the pots empty and a shiny trail to add insult to injury. When the plants are about six inches tall they are ready to be planted out to their permanent location.

Planting Out

THE CHOICE OF GROWING SITE WILL OBVIOUSLY BE PERSONAL but a sheltered south-facing slope is ideal. If the plants are to be grown in the wild then they will need protection from rabbits etc. Surround the plot with a 1 inch mesh wire-netting fence dug 6 inches into the ground, and at least 3 feet high, supported with bamboo poles. When digging in the wire-netting try and angle the bottom of the wire outwards. This will make it more difficult for rabbits to scratch their way in. Wherever the location, the ground will need preparation. This will depend on the condition and type of the soil and whether it has been previously cultivated.

What does the plant require of the soil? It needs to breathe through it, feed from it, drink from it and anchor itself in it. So the soil needs to be porous, contain plant food, be moist and be firm. Humus which is either decayed farmyard manure, compost or leaf mold is essential, as this supplies food and aerates the soil. The three essential nutrients for plant growth are Nitrate, Phosphate and Potash. Nitrate builds up leaves and stems, Phosphates develop root growth and hasten ripening of flowers and seeds, Potash makes for hardy growth and resistance to disease.

The three essential nutrients for plant growth are Nitrate, Phosphate and Potash

Lime is also used in soil preparation. It sweetens the soil, i.e. it reduces the acidity of the soil. Lime is applied as a dusting in the winter and is washed into the ground by the action of rain. Compost, manure or organic fertiliser should never be applied at the same time as lime, as they will react with each other. There are also trace elements necessary for healthy plant growth, but as these will normally be present in the ground they will not be dealt with here.

A list of trace elements and deficiency signs is given in appendix 1, but always check the soil before making any changes as an acid soil will produce many symptoms of soil deficiency.

The relative acidity or alkalinity of the soil is known as the pH and is measured on a scale of 0 acid to 14 alkaline. Cannabis will grow in soils with a pH of 5 to 8.5 but thrives in nearly neutral soils with a pH of 7 to 8, so it is important to know the pH of the soil you are planting in. It can vary greatly in a given area, so it is worth investing in a test kit. They are relatively inexpensive, easy to use and will ensure that you give the plants the best medium in which to grow. Generally soils tend to be acid rather than alkaline.

Let's assume that the land to be used has not been cultivated for some time and go through the stages of preparation. In the late

autumn, cut back long grass, brambles etc. and skim off the surface to a depth of 1-2 inches and stack to one side. This stack will break down through the winter and can be spread back over the ground in the spring. Dig soil to a spade depth, removing every bit you can see of the roots of permanent weeds. Give a good dusting of lime, about 1lb. per square yard, and leave until the early spring. On very alkaline soils, the lime won't be necessary. If the plot requires netting-in, do so at this time. Do a good job, as rabbits will find any weak spots and work away until they are in. There is nothing more depressing than returning to a plot and finding a few stalks where fine young plants should be. In dry seasons they are particularly persistent, so be warned!

In the early spring dig the plot over again removing any weeds and add compost, well-rotted farmyard or stable manure. Turn this in to the top few inches of the soil. There are concentrated manures available from garden centres which are up to six times stronger than regular aged farmyard manure. These make life easier when plots are off in the wilds! Remember that the plants need to Breathe, Feed, and Drink and Anchor themselves down in the ground and you will have the plant's best interests in mind.

Chemical fertilisers can be used, but if the soil is very light it is best to try and give the soil substance by adding humus (compost or manure). If the plot is on sloping ground, it is worth terracing to prevent the run-off of rain. The terracing can be carefully done to retain as much rainfall as possible in dry years. Form each level of the terrace with a raised outer edge to hold the rain and slope each level so any overflow will pass to the next level, and so on down to the bottom level, just like the Incas.

Be sure to firm down the soil, especially the outside edges of the terraces. This will help to retain moisture in the ground. Obviously, if the ground tends to be wet then try and loosen the ground which will aerate the soil and help the plants breathe.

There will be warmth in the soil and the young plants will be ready to go out to their permanent location

Soils are 'hungry' when water drains through them quickly, removing nutrients, especially nitrogen and potassium. Organic foods are really important on hungry sandy soils, as they stay in the vicinity of the roots longer, so plenty of humus. Gypsum and Dolomite will help in improving water-holding power. Lasting nutritional benefit can be given to the land by the addition of Rock Potash at a half-a-pound per square yard, and Rock Phosphate at one pound per square yard. This will give benefit to light sandy soils for several years.

Hopefully after all this preparation Spring will have arrived, there will be warmth in the soil and the young plants will be ready to go out to their permanent location. If the location is out in the wilds then they can be transported in lidded plastic buckets, as used in beer-making. As a matter of interest, two buckets will fit one on top of the other into a large backpack, allowing the transportation of thirty plants. If there is no transportation involved then plants can be allowed to get larger before transplanting, but don't let them get pot-bound or growth will be stunted. Before transplanting, give the plants a good watering and feed. Seaweed extract is an excellent choice of organic nutrient. It's not a bad idea to also give them a spray of insecticide to discourage aphids that love young tender growth. I give a light dusting, using an aerosol spray.

Break away some of the side of the pot to prevent the pot shrinking away from the surrounding soil, causing the plant to become stunted.

Carefully place remaining pot and rootball in ground.

Plant out using a trowel to make a hole in the ground the size of the peat pot. Take the plant in its peat pot and break away some of the side of the pot, exposing the roots. If this is not done and the weather is dry, there is a chance that the pot will shrink away from the surrounding soil, trapping the roots in the pot and stunting the plants growth. Although some root damage will occur by doing this, recovery will be swift. Press the remaining pot and root ball into the hole and firm down the surrounding soil. Space the plants at about two-foot six-inch centres, although this can vary depending on the season. If a dry season is expected and plants will be small, then plant closer together. A handful of fish blood and bone meal can be spread around the plants and allowed to be washed in by rain.

Problems that can be encountered during the early days are attack by slugs and snails. Use slug pellets and scatter them around before planting. Aphids can cause major damage, so keep an eye out as they multiply fast. They will be dealt with along with other pests when the plants are foliar fed. The other main problem encountered is the ground starting to dry out before the roots have gained depth. If you feel the soil is a bit dry at planting-time, then it is worth watering the plants in and making sure the soil is well firmed down. Once the roots have gained deeper, moister ground the plant will survive. Later watering is not recommended, as this will encourage growth that will sap the plant's strength if dry weather continues.

The fact is that once you start watering you will have to continue until there is a substantial rainfall, which of course might be a long time coming. Providing the plants go in at the right time nature will take care of growth. Keep the plot clear of weeds. In dry weather, hoe around the plants to make a

Firm down the surrounding soil. Make sure it is good and firm. Finally loosen up just the surface, this will form a barrier to prevent moisture loss.

dust mulch. This will make a barrier against water evaporation from the soil.

Foliar feeding using a garden sprayer is highly recommended. Different 'cocktails' can be made up to cover the plant's needs at different stages of growth. During the early stages the plant is making leaf and stem, which requires a feed containing high Nitrogen, medium Phosphate and Potash. There are chemical fertilisers available which are balanced to give the best feed at different stages of growth. These are marked with an N.P.K. value (N Nitrogen, P Phosphate, K Potash), so for the early feed an N.P.K. value of 25:15:15 is ideal. To get rid of any pests that might attack the plants, an insecticide can be added to the foliar feed. A fungicide can also be added during damp weather, or if mould is discovered. Make up the dilutions as recommended by the manufacturer and spray over and under leaves giving a good wetting. Also give the base of the stem a squirt, this will kill any frog-hopper nymphs that tend to lurk at soil level. They also appear on leaves in spittle-like cocoons. Do not spray in bright sunshine as this can damage leaves. To aid in the adhesion of the spray to the plant, add a drop of washing-up liquid to the mix. Make sure all mixes are compatible, by following the manufacturers' recommendations.

For those who want the organic approach, there are seaweed extract feeds available. A natural insecticide/fungicide which is also beneficial to the plant, as it leaves behind Potassium and Manganese (trace elements required for healthy growth) is Potassium Permanganate. It kills aphids and discourages moulds, but should not be used after the tenth week of the plants' development, as an excess of potassium will have a negative effect on resin production. Dissolve the crystals in a jam-jar of warm water, use at a rate of seven grams of crystals per gallon of spray. After spraying with Potassium Permanganate the plants will be an odd reddish colour, but relax, they will soon be green again and healthier for the experience. After the tenth week use a proprietary brand of insecticide and fungicide. Foliar feed every ten to fourteen days. The spray needs to be absorbed by the plant, so if rain is expected it is better to wait for a dry spell.

If chemical fertiliser is being used, and as spring changes to early summer, the feed can be changed from a 25:15:15 mix to a 20:20:20 mix. This will only be used for a short time, until say mid to late June when it will change to a 12.5:25:25 mix. The 25 Phosphate will encourage the plant to flower, early flowering being one of our main objectives. The 25 Potash gives resistance to disease and encourages hardy growth.

The organic alternative can be Fish meal and Bone meal sprinkled round the base of the plant and watered in, and a foliar feed of seaweed extract. Whatever methods are being used, keep the plot clear of weeds so air can circulate round the plants. This will reduce the chance of attack by moulds that love still, damp air.

> Also give the base of the stem a squirt, this will kill any frog-hopper nymphs that tend to lurk at soil level.

Sexing and Flowering

THE IDEAL TIME FOR THE PLANTS TO DECLARE THEIR sex is around the beginning of July. As mentioned before, in the U.K. the longest day is 21st. of June, with about 18 hours of daylight, which is not conducive to flowering. So some previous acclimatization will have to have taken place, or the blackout technique will have to be used.

Usually the male plant will be the first to declare its sex. Pubescent flowers can develop on the main stem, at the third or fourth node from the top of the plant. (Illustration following page). The discovery of these flowers will give an indication of future male plants, but is not definitive. If by this time the plot is in need of thinning out, then removing plants with pubescent male flowers can give future female plants more space.

Pubescent female flowers can also appear on a potential female plant in the same way as on the males. They form in the same location, but instead of a petalled flower forming, the small pod develops without the slim stem, and two white pistils form at the end of the pod (see detail in illustration).

Pollen can be painted on to female flower heads using a fine artists brush

For seed production, a male will have to be allowed to pollinate a female, so making a good choice of parents is important. For the British climate, strains with a more open structure are preferable to 'poker style' more densely-formed plants, as the former are less prone to attract moulds during the flowering stage. So make your choice carefully: it will be a compromise between early flowering and genetic type. This criteria applies to both male and female. When a suitable male and female have been chosen, allow the female to develop until white pistils are visible and well developed in the flower heads. Take the male,

which should be in full flowering mode, with open flowers and yellow pollen visible. Dust the female with the male flower heads and pollination should occur. Natural air movement will normally perform this task, but the above method should allow for more selective pollination. Pollen can be collected in a clear plastic bag and selectively painted on to specific female flower heads, using a fine artist's brush. If you try and store pollen to use on later flowering females, keep it as dry as possible as it tends to degrade very quickly.

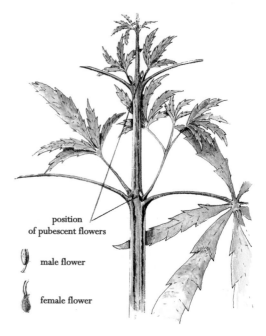

position
of pubescent flowers

male flower

female flower

In practical terms, to get a seed crop and produce good Sinsemilla in the same plot requires all the male plants to be removed before the main flowering of the females. This will mean frequent inspection during the flowering period. Although males do tend to flower ahead of the females, late flowering males that you were convinced were going to be females do appear. It only takes one to sex your whole plot and its good-bye Sinsemilla halloo seeds!

So allow a selected male to flower at the same time as your earliest decent-looking females that are showing their first pistils. Give the male a good shake-about to distribute the pollen, then remove the male and any future males that appear. If you have timed it right you will have produced some early seed in a plot of plants that is for the most part seedless.

Although Cannabis plants are normally either male or female, they can sometimes become hermaphrodite, i.e. produce both male and female flowers on the same plant. This usually happens on late-flowering females, with the appearance of male flowers in the female flower clusters. These rogue male flowers tend to be more yellow than the flowers of regular males. It has been suggested

Two young plants — the plant on the left shows an open structure, as opposed to the plant on the right, which has a more dense form. These would be ideal partners for producing a new strain.

that seed produced by predominantly female hermaphrodite plants will produce all female seed, but as these tend to be late-flowering there seems little point in using them. If you find a lot of hermaphrodite plants, it is a sign that the plants are suffering from some form of stress. This could be due to soil condition or external conditions, but it indicates that something is amiss. Personally it is not something I would want to see appear. My advice is not to use seed from hermaphrodite plants.

Continue with the foliar feeding, using the high phosphate/potash mix, and watch out for gray and brown moulds (Botrytis Cinerea). These appear generally in late summer and can be very destructive, spreading very fast in damp weather. They form on stems and buds, and have a dry, dusty appearance, but are wet inside. Clean the mould away, and remove rotted growth. Give an extra squirt of foliar spray mix, containing a fungicide, and pray for dry weather. Carbendazim is a specific cure for this type of mould. As the plants use considerable amounts of food during flowering, it's worth sprinkling a handful of fish and bone meal around each plant and lightly hoeing in.

Also as the plants develop towards maturity the large fan leaves, which have been responsible for the conversion of sunlight into energy, will start to turn yellow and drop. This will continue right through till harvest-time and it can be advantageous to remove the dead leaves from the plant to aid in air circulation. Do it before foliar feeding but be careful not to damage the plant by pulling them off too early.

This page; Male showing open flower which will release pollen to air movement, sexing any surrounding females.

Opposite page; Female at suitable stage of development for pollination (sexing).

Opposite page main picture; Shows a male plant with an open growth structure. This plant was used for selective pollination on specific females.

Above left; Shows a late flowering male plant with a compact growth structure, also used for selective pollination on specific females.

Above right and centre; Two different strains of female, both were sexed and used for selective seed production.

Harvesting

THE BIG QUESTION IS, WHEN TO HARVEST?
THIS WILL vary from year to year, depending on what sort of summer it has been. Hopefully it's been a brilliant summer and everything has gone according to plan. The female flower heads will have swollen considerably, and in the last week of development will have become quite firm. Development can be considered finished when the pistils have

Although under some conditions, especially long hot summers (rare we know), the lower branches can develop ahead of the upper.

gone a tobacco colour. There should be a white dusting of resin on the inner leaves of the flower-heads. Not all the flower heads will ripen at exactly the same time, so the best method is to crop the tops of individual plants, and allow the lower branches to finish development before they too are cropped.

Use a pair of snips or sharp knife, being careful not to lose any seeds if the plant has been seeded. A good indication that the plant is finished is a yellowing of the stems, which should also have become hollow. If the harvested plants have to be transported from an outside plot, it is worth cutting

Opposite page left; Plot at planting stage to show relative size of plot.

Opposite page right; Early stage of growth.
Note small plant in foreground, this was a replacement plant for an early male which was removed.

This page left; Plants at mid stage of development.

This page right; Getting close to harvest.
Note yellowing of fan leaves.

can start at the end of July, with the very early varieties continuing until the end of September. Usually the weather has deteriorated by the beginning of October and no benefit will be gained by leaving plants out any longer.

Care should be taken to keep a record of all seeds harvested, indicating parent-plant type and date cropped. If records are kept, different strains can be crossed and specific genetic improvement can be made. This of course will be decided on personal preferences and local conditions, but

the stems to a length that will fit into a backpack, then bunching them and placing carefully in a plastic bin-bag which is then slid into the backpack. This will help prevent damage to the buds and keep the stems fresh for processing. Depending on the variety and variation of strains, cropping

primarily getting an early strain is the most important factor. Although you think you will remember which seeds are which at the time, when it comes time to germinate again you will have nagging doubts as to just what is what. So Keep Records.

Drying

THE METHOD OF DRYING WILL DEPEND ON THE VOLUME of plants being processed, but the technique for manicuring each plant is basically the same. The fan leaves are removed first and the ends of the growing leaves around the flowering buds are also removed. The best technique is to hold the stem in one hand and working from the bottom up, snap back on the stalks of the fan leaves, using the thumb and first finger of the other hand. Once the fan leaves are gone it's much easier to see what else needs to be removed. Use the thumb and first finger to get in to the base of each flowering head and remove the smaller sun leaves. Also remove the tips of the

The sequence of stem manicure

1
Complete stem

2
Removal of fan leaves

3
Tips of leaves removed

Opposite page;
A picked down stem showing what has been removed.
Note yellow fan leaves, a sign of a mature plant..

surrounding leaves to expose the flower clusters. It's much easier to perform this first stage of manicuring before the plant starts to wilt. This can be delayed by putting the harvested plants in a bin-bag, in a cool place.

Top above; manicured stems hung on stretched wire in drying room, note removed buds on mesh rack with dehumidifier underneath.

Above; buds being removed from stems.

After trimming, the processed stems should be hung in a dry airy space, out of direct sunlight, and allowed to dry slowly over several days. The most important aspect of the initial drying process is that the moisture is drawn slowly from the stem into the middle of the flower clusters, and out through the flower ends. If drying is done too quickly, the flower ends will become crisped and disintegrate before all the moisture is out of the flower centres. The stems can be hung on stretched plastic-covered garden wire, which makes it easy to slide them into bunches to slow down drying, or spread them out to speed up the process. If dealing with fairly large volumes, keep an eye out for moulds, which can develop quickly if there is poor air circulation. A dehumidifier is very useful for removing moisture, and can allow for a controlled drying period in conjunction with temperature control. The higher the temperature, the faster moisture will be removed. The buds can be removed from the stems using a pair of trimming snips. These are actually seamstress's scissors available from sewing shops. They can also be used to manicure the

The higher the temperature, the faster moisture will be removed

buds if connoisseur quality is required. Once the buds are removed from the stems, they can be laid out on a rack of fine-mesh garden netting. Again, they can be spread out or bunched up to control the rate of drying.

When you feel that the buds are fairly dry, transfer them to a supermarket-style plastic bag. Compress the buds down in the bag to exclude as much air as possible, but not enough to damage the structure of the buds. Twist the top of the bag down, compressing the contents, and tie. In this compressed state any moisture that is left will be evenly distributed through the bag. After a day or two, open the bag and feel for any moisture. If any dampness is felt, transfer back to the mesh rack. Be careful at this stage not to over-dry and crisp the crop. At this final stage of drying I tend to repeat the process of transferring from drying rack to plastic bag several times, drawing the moisture out over a period of about a week. This makes for a much smoother quality product. Finally, store in airtight containers extracting as much air as possible before sealing, and keep in a cool dry location. I always check

Be careful at this stage not to over dry and crisp the crop

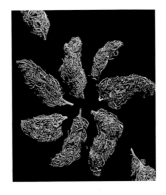
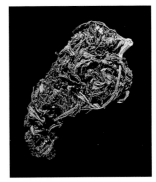

everything for dampness after a couple of weeks, and if all is well figure that storage will be good for at least six months to a year. If a fairly substantial amount is being stored, then plastic bags containing a pound or so, packed in sealable buckets and stored in a cool place will deteriorate very little over a period of a year. A few silica crystals placed in the bottom of the bucket will soak up any trace-moisture present.

That about sums it up. The following is a diary of events, and the various ups and downs encountered in one particular year. All that remains is to wish "Good Luck" to anyone who has a go! The buds shown above were produced in that "one particular year".

Diary of a season

Germination and planting dates

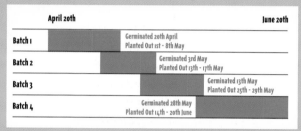

	April 20th				June 20th
Batch 1			Germinated 20th April Planted Out 1st - 8th May		
Batch 2				Germinated 3rd May Planted Out 13th - 17th May	
Batch 3					Germinated 13th May Planted Out 25th - 29th May
Batch 4			Germinated 28th May Planted Out 14th - 20th June		

THIS PARTICULAR YEAR WAS COMPLETELY DIFFERENT from the previous year, which had a warm gentle spring. This was the opposite. The wind blew from the east for most of April, the air was cold and the ground was very dry. There was a good fall of rain on the 18th of May. Previous to that there had been no rain for about 5 weeks. There were a few sunny days after the 19th May then a little more rain. The temperature started to rise, with dull misty days until the end of May. The first planting-out of seedlings went into ground that was really too cold to encourage strong growth. The second planting-out fared a little better. The ground had sufficient moisture, and the soil had warmed up a little. By the time of the third planting-out, the ground was again very dry, which stopped root development and caused the plants to stunt. This particular spring had some of the most extreme weather conditions I can remember. Without the staggered plantings, the year would have been doomed to failure.

While planting the third back-up batch into an outside plot, some very early males were spotted. The hard spring and adverse weather conditions had triggered the sex and survive centre in the plants' metabolism. The plants,

only 18 inches or so high, were removed and replaced with plants from the third batch germinated. The weather remained poor, with dull overcast days and below average temperatures. June started wet, gloom and doom was the order of the day as last year's stash shrank, and the thought of running out was close to becoming a reality.

By the end of the second week in June the sun was shining, with daytime temperatures in the seventies, and spring, or rather the lack of a spring, was turning to summer. Of the three batches of plants put out the majority were looking very stunted. Some of the second batch were looking O.K. but generally things were looking bad. At the beginning of June some of the third batch of seedlings in the greenhouse had their light reduced to eight hours a day, and within two weeks were showing their sex, the idea being to fill the vacant spaces left by the removal of the male plants with guaranteed female plants. These were actions of a desperate grower faced with a stunted crop. As it turned out, these plants generally performed very badly. The stress of having the light reduced, followed by a return to an 18hr. day, caused the plants to deform and show hermaphrodite tendencies. As I've said, this is not something that one would want to introduce to the seed strain.

A very small number of these stressed plants did do well, showing no abnormalities. The few seeds obtained from these were saved, to be used for further experimentation.

All the plants were sprayed with an insecticide, fungicide and foliar feed cocktail during the second week of June. If anything can save a plant, foliar feeding is the one, that is if the mix is good! This time it wasn't, so the already suffering plants had their leaves burned by too strong a spray. The larger, more healthy plants took about a week to recover and show fresh growth, but the more stunted plants looked sad.

The long-range weather forecast at the end of June predicted rain, which offered a glimmer of hope, so a more careful, very mild foliar feed was given on the 23rd and 27th of June. This definitely helped. On the 29th June there were light showers with the promise of a gale of wind and more rain to follow.

The seedlings from the fourth batch germinated were planted in plots that had emergency water stashes and were watered in. This was done during the last week of June, in anticipation of the forecast rain. If plots are out in the wilds, it's vital to conceal any trails, which makes humping water or making too many visits inadvisable. So an emergency water stash can save the day. This can be a plastic dustbin which should hold about 30 gallons or so. Providing it is open to the sky, normal rainfall should fill it during the course of the year. It is sometimes better to let the plants struggle and remain small and use the water when rain is expected. In this situation nutrients can be added which would give the plants a boost. When the conditions are right, plants can make growth like "Jack's beanstalk." You can almost watch them grow.

4th July. After a week of showery, windy weather, the plants were foliar fed with a spray of potassium permanganate mixed with a 20-20-20 NPK. chemical feed. After this the mix was changed to 12.5-25-25. This change would normally have occurred earlier, but this was a very late year. Some more male plants were removed, and in one plot a nice-looking male was left to provide pollen for the earliest females. It was removed before the main flowering of the females. The plants were still very small because of the drought, but the little rain that fell left some moisture in the ground, so all was not yet lost.

13th July. For the previous week the weather was generally showery, with dull humid days, so the foliar feeding included a fungicide. Some early sexed females that were kept in a greenhouse were in their final stage of seed production, and were showing signs of mould, so they were dusted with Bordeaux powder. In a closed environment such as a greenhouse where there is limited air movement, using a liquid fungicide can actually do more harm than good. A dry powder such as Bordeaux is better as it introduces no extra moisture, but I would definitely not recommend using it on plant material that is to be consumed as it contains copper compounds. Take the plant out of the greenhouse and dust outside. The weather remained variable for the remainder of July and into the beginning of August. On the 10th August some early females were cropped. They could have done with a few more days of ripening, which would have allowed the buds to firm up a bit more, but as they were showing signs of mould the decision was taken to crop. As it turned out, about an hour after cropping the plants, the heavens opened delivering both torrential rain and hailstones. Also in the first two weeks

A dry powder called Bordeaux is better as it introduces no extra moisture.

of August, the early greenhouse females, which had been lightly dusted with selected male pollen, were cropped. One of these females (which had shown the least signs of mould and was also the nicest looking), was put to one side and dried separately. The seed from this plant was labelled "Best greenhouse plant", dated and stored for next year's effort. Seed from the other greenhouse females was dated, labelled "Stock greenhouse seed" and also stored.

After the deluge, and contrary to "The Weathermen", the sun shone for the next week. From the 16th to the 20th August all the plants were sprayed, and more plants were cropped. Again a few signs of mould were present, but as the weather was quite humid this was to be expected. Considering how badly the year had begun, and the very poor spring, things were looking a lot better than had been expected.

The drying process was commenced in earnest on the 20th of August, when a sizeable cropping took place, and a happy smile started to creep across my face. Although the weather remained showery, the daytime temperature stayed up around 70 degrees, and a sizeable cropping took place on the 27th August. Very little mould was present, the spraying having paid off, and several of the remaining plants were standing tall at about seven feet, with firm solid buds.

From the beginning of September until the final cropping on the 12th September, the weather remained dry and sunny. The last croppings produced some of the best looking and strongest buds. Considering the very poor spring and early summer, a better than expected crop was produced. The plants were sprayed every ten days or so during the growing period, with appropriate mixes for the particular stage of growth. This definitely improved the growth of the plants when conditions were harsh.

For the final flowering process, the daytime temperature remained around the 70 degree mark, which enabled the buds to fully mature. All in all it was an extremely hard year, with smaller than average plants, but thanks to the excellent weather in the late summer, the quality was first rate. It must be emphasized that these are very hardy plants, extremely adaptable, and will always give of their best if given half a chance.

Appendix 1

TRACE ELEMENTS ESSENTIAL TO PLANT GROWTH

Boron For development of strong stem tissue. In plant foods.

Calcium Is connected with the development of leaf clusters. Source bone meal.

Chlorine Lack of affects root system. Deficiency very uncommon.

Iron Is connected with Photosynthesis and respiration. In plant foods.

Magnesium Part of plants Chlorophyll (Green). Source Epsom salts

Molybdenum Essential for nitrogen fixation. Lacking in many soils. Symptoms yellowing of leaves between veins, starts toward middle of plant spreads to younger leaves which become twisted. Use plant food containing this trace element.

Sulphur Lack of, unusual, causes yellowing of younger leaves. Source Sulphate.

Zinc Connected with leaf development. In specific plant foods.

Appendix 2

CUTTINGS FROM GREENHOUSE PLANTS

It is possible to take cuttings from female plants that have declared their sex and are in the very early stages of producing pistils. If the taller, more stretched females being grown in the greenhouse are pinched out to encourage the development of more growing tips, then these growing tips can later be used for cuttings.

The best technique is to pick a cool day, spray the plant with water (which will slow down wilting), and with a scalpel or very sharp knife cut the growing stem at a distance from the tip of about 2.5 to 3 inches. Immediately stand the cuttings in water, this will also discourage wilting. Have prepared the required number of cutting cells. These are available from garden centres and come in strips or trays. The cells should be filled with a mix comprising of one half compost and the other half vermiculite and perlite in equal quantities. Firm this mix well down into the cells, and give a good watering. It is better for cuttings if the mix is well compressed. To help the cutting take, use a rooting powder or gel, again available from garden centres. The powder variety usually has a dibber for making a hole in the filled growing cells. Take the cutting from the water, trim off any leaves below the growing tip, dip the bottom half-inch of the cutting in the rooting compound and place as deep as possible in the growing cells. Firm down the growing medium and repeat for the rest of the cuttings. Give the transplanted cuttings another spray of water and place in the propagator. The propagator should be kept in the shade at a temperature of around 70 degrees F. and the cuttings should be sprayed with water regularly to prevent wilting. After about ten days roots should start to form and the top of the propagator can be removed and the cuttings given more direct light. Any sign of wilting indicates that either roots are not yet supporting the plant or the leaves have been allowed to dry out. When the cuttings have rooted, they can be transferred to growing trays or flower pots and grown on. Once established these cuttings will grow very quickly and can produce excellent results.

Some thoughts on the use of cannabis

Archeological evidence indicates that Cannabis first grew in central Asia. The Scythians, a nomadic tribe originating in Siberia, are credited with introducing the plant to many parts of the middle-east and Europe from 1500 BC. onwards.

The earliest mention of the plant appears in the text of the Atharvaveda, around 300 BC. The name given was Bhang, a liquid concoction that could be used externally or internally. There was a sacredness associated with the use of Bhang which has continued in India until the present day. References in Indian literature to the smoking of cannabis, either in its natural form called ganja, or processed into solid form Known as Charas, appear much later. It is then that the debate as to the moral good of the plant appears. The habit of using this herb with Tobacco brought its use into further disrepute.

In the UK, following the Indian tradition, Cannabis is most often smoked with the dreaded killer weed tobacco. This is really the most unfortunate aspect of the whole business.

Obviously the social acceptance of any mind stimulating substance will change as more and more of society become involved. I believe that cannabis has found, in the modern western culture, a ready audience for the magic it can perform. Unlike alcohol with its chemical poisons, it is a natural creation. In the same way as one should approach food and eat a healthy organic diet, any intake for the mind should follow the same code . I think this approach will be some time coming. In the States dope is generally smoked without the addition of tobacco, one Americanism that Europe could do well to adopt. For the time being, it would appear that cannabis is going to continue to affect society and contribute changes to the way we behave. No amount of laws will stop people enjoying the feeling of getting high. The real world has become, for many, a very hostile environment with little scope for wealth or success. Dope-smoking takes the edge off this harsh life and generally seems to enhance the better side of man.

On the other hand, there is a wealthy elite who have a lot of everything and move so fast they don't really have time to be aware of the 'other half'. If these elite are successful they end up retiring off somewhere and sticking their heads up their vested interests. Their successors continue to burn natural resources at an alarming rate. There is no blame in these observations, human nature is what it is, some are successful and some are not. What is of interest is that the indulgence of the successful is Cocaine and the fix of the desperate is Crack. Both very expensive, addictive and very destructive.

Having spent so many years enjoying the company of cannabis, I would like to pass on a few observations. For me, the very best for the brain is naturally grown weed, fed on natural sunshine and natural organic food. There is no need for it to be the tropics, cannabis can adapt to almost any conditions. Growing is an exchange between man and plant, and should be done with love. Exploitation brings bad results.

For most young people today, I think dope-smoking is a socially acceptable pursuit, and I think there is a live-and-let-live attitude between those that do and those that don't. Instead of the 'Powers that be' fighting to alienate sub-cultures with propaganda there should be an understanding as to why so many people feel the need to share this common bond. Like all social interactions, there is always a foundation-stone from which the activity spreads. The foundation stone of the dope-smoker is a plant known from earliest times to be medicinal. A plant used in spiritual endeavours, and respected by holy men in many different cultures.

ABOUT GROWING UNDER LIGHTS
I have never undertaken this method of cultivation, being fortunate in having a good outside environment. My main concern about this method is more for the plants than those that will consume them. Most artificial environments I have seen remind me of "battery chicken production". All a bit soulless, lights on lights off, lights on lights

off etc. Some very strong smoke is produced this way, but to me it inherits the buzz of the lights. It switches you on then switches you off. There is no dawn no dusk, no sunrise no sunset. No season, no storms, no rain, no clouds, no subtle changes. I suppose it really depends on the importance one attaches to being in contact with nature. Technology tends to separate man from nature, but without it how will we be able to cultivate our gardens on the moon when the time comes? There is nothing to say that plant life is any less adaptable to artificial environments than man himself.

For me though, being a bit of a nature boy, the big outdoors with all its variables is where it's at. It has given me a better understanding of the environment and a respect of nature. Learning to accept what nature hands out, the bad years as well as the good years.

The secretive nature of the guerrilla grower's activity, minimizes the amount of disturbance that is made in any growing area. Birds and animals are undisturbed and the feeling grows of being part of nature. The pleasure of arriving at a secret garden around harvest time, from a hidden trial that no one has discovered and seeing beautiful healthy plants swaying in the breeze is immense. The sun sends no electricity bills, burns no fossil fuels and causes no pollution. There is a poem which sums it all up.

The kiss of the sun for pardon

The song of a bird for mirth

You are closer to God in a garden

Than anywhere else on earth.

Of course it can happen that disaster strikes and all ones efforts are lost. This can be from what are generally known as "Rippers" those too lazy to grow their own. Or even worse those upholders of the law who, when they find a plot, go in like bulldozers and cause destruction on a major scale. It takes a strong will to come to terms with such losses, there is nothing that can be done in view of the illegal nature of the crop.

It must be remembered that the repercussions of being caught growing Marijuana can be severe, LOSS OF LIBERTY being the worst. A criminal record which can cost you your job, stop you travelling abroad, and cause untold problems to family life.

At the time of writing, the feeling is, that there is a certain tolerance towards the cultivation of marijuana especially if it is to be used for therapeutic purposes, but this can vary from place to place and time to time. Until legalisation occurs be careful!

There is just one more thing which I feel I should pass on, regarding the health aspect of smoking. As it says on the carton Smoking Damages Health. So it comes down to balancing between what is good for your head, and what is good for your body. Tobacco is definitely a killer, so if possible avoid mixing it with weed. I know it's what everybody does, but be an individual and save yourself the health hazard. It took me until I was 40 years old to give up. When you're young you think nothing can get you, but believe me it can and it will. Your lungs and your heart will suffer in later life. You only have one body and one life, so treat it well. It is also much easier to take a break from smoking if you smoke your weed neat. Cannabis is definitely not as addictive as tobacco, so many people say "Oh I don't smoke cigarettes, I smoke joints" which somehow lets them off the fact that really they have a tobacco problem. So I would say if you have an addictive personality, as I do, get off the tobacco habit. Good Luck and God Bless.

Medicinal use of Marijuana

In June 1998 a license was granted to a pharmaceutical company in the U.K. to grow, possess and supply cannabis for research purposes. In November of the same year The House of Lords Science and Technology Select Committee published a report entitled, Cannabis the Scientific and Medical Evidence. Recommendations were made that there should be clinical trials of cannabis for the treatment of MS and cronic pain and research should begin into methods of administration, which would retain the fast action obtained by inhalation. It was also recommended that Cannabis should be reclassified as a schedule 2 Drug, to enable doctors to prescribe an appropriate preparation of cannabis on a named-patient basis. Even though these recommendations were turned down by the government, the first "licenced crop" for twenty-five years has been harvested and the first clinical trials using a cannabinoid extract and focusing on patients with MS and nerve damage, are about to begin.

Although the government would prefer to synthesize and standardize the active ingredients of marijuana, there is anecdotal and scientific evidence that the proportion of active ingredients (cannabinoids and THC) change during the final development of the bud. This would account for the various "highs" experienced when different sorts of marijuana are smoked. These differences are important when the plant is being used for medicinal purposes. The recent discovery of cannabinoid receptors in the human body would seem to verify the need for further research.

In the meantime, thousands of sufferers of a variety of complaints who reject the chemicals prescribed by their doctors, continue to put themselves at risk, by using marijuana to ease their suffering. For someone who has suffered a lifetime of chronic pain, from a specific complaint, and finds purely by experience, that marijuana can help him through an otherwise desperate life, there is no option but to use it. From personal experience the chemical alternative prescribed by doctors has a far more damaging effect on the body and mind.

Seeds Plants & Buds

All grown outside in the UK and maturing from early August to the beginning of September.